LABORATORY MANUAL ON BIOTECHNOLOGY AND BIOCHEMISTRY

KRISHANU

DEDICATED TO OUR PARENTS

Contents

Preface

The Manual "Biochemistry and Biotechnology" has been written as per the syllabus of B.Tech. and B.Sc Biotechnology students.

The manual is an introduction to basic techniques of Biochemistry and Biotechnology. It covers basic topicsas qualitative and quantitative analysis of carbohydrates, proteins, enzyme kinetics and chromatographic methods. The chemical composition of all reagents is provided along with experiments to enable students to understand basic reactions of biomolecules.

We wish to express our deep sense of gratitude to Prof R.S Sengar HOD Ag Biotech SVPUAT, Prof R Kumar, DEAN COB and Prof Pankaj Kumar, Head of MEB and Bioinformatics for their inspiring guidance, constant encouragement and continuous support.

We are grateful to various authors and publishers for consultation during preparation of the manual. We are thankful to our colleagues, Poornima Maurya, Santosh Kumar, Veer Pratap Singh and well wishers for their consistent encouragement.

We cordially invite suggestions from users for further improvement of the manual.

Content

LIST OF EXPERIMENTS

1. General guidelines for working in biochemistry lab.
2. To prepare the solutions with given concentration (0.1M glucose, 0.15M NaCl, 1% NaCl, 0.5N NaOH).
3. Normal value of constituents in biological fluids.
4. To perform calibration of pH electrode.
5. To detect the presence of monosaccharide with the help of Molish's reagent.
6. To study the properties of carbohydrate with the help of Fehling's solution.
7. To detect the presence of reducing sugar with the help of Benedict's reagent.
8. Identification and separation of amino acid by Thin layer Chromatography (TLC).
9. To estimate the protein content in bovine serum albumin (BSA) by Bradford method.
10. Estimation of the amount of reducing sugar in the unknown sample by DNS method.
11. Estimation of the amount of protein in the unknown sample by Lowry method.
12. Estimation of the amount of protein in the unknown sample by Biuret method.
13. Estimation of the amount of RNA in the unknown sample by Orcinol method.
14. Estimation of the amount of DNA in the unknown sample by DPA method.
15. Estimation of RNA content by orcinol method.

CHAPTER ONE

General instructions for working in Biochemistry lab.

1. Care and cleanliness must be practiced by the laboratory personnel at all times.
2. Bottles should never be carried by neck when transporting from one part to other part of the laboratory.
3. Trays should be used to carry reagents.
4. If corrosive, poisonous liquids are being thrown down the sink, they should be accompanied by a generous supply of water to ensure by the time they reach the main drain, they will be too dilute to be dangerous.
5. Organic solvents being inflammable should not be stored near electricity sockets.
6. Care should be taken to ensure that all gas taps works efficiently and that no gas escapes when the taps turned off.
7. Don't attempt to find gas leaks by using lighting matches.
8. Electric switch and connections should be repeatedly inspected and kept free from corrosion, so that no danger shocks arise from short circuiting or due to exposure of naked wire resulting from breaking of insulation.
9. When a laboratory is to be left unattended and any length of time all gas and water taps should be turned off.
10. Paper should never be used to carry the light from one burner to other.
11. Insoluble waste should not be thrown into the sink.
12. While working in a laboratory, wear a protective coat.
13. When dealing with volatile inflammable liquids, no flame should be allowed in the vicinity.
14. In case of emergency, medical attention should be quickly sought.

CHAPTER TWO

EXPERIMENT NO. 1

AIM: To prepare the solutions with given concentration (0.1M glucose, 0.15M NaCl, 1% NaCl, 0.5N NaOH).

REQUIREMENTS:

Beaker (250 ml), conical flask (100 ml), measuring cylinder (50-100 ml), glucose, nail, NaOH, volumetric flask, pipettes.

PRINCIPLE:

A solution is defined as a homogenous mixture of two or more substances, the composition of which may vary within certain limits. The components of a solution may be defined as the solvent and the solutes.

CONCENTRATION EXPRESSIONS:

MOLARITY:

The molarity (M) of a solution is the number of moles of solute in 1 litre (L) of the solution.

MOLALITY:

The molality of a solution is the number of moles of solute in 1000 gm of solvent.

PERCENTAGE EXPRESSIONS:

Percent expressions are commonly used to express the concentrations of solutions. These include,

a. Percentage weight – in – volume (%w/v) expresses the number of grams (g) of constituents in 100 ml of solution.
b. Percentage weight – in – weight (%w/w) expresses the number of grams (g) of constituents in 100 g of solution.

NORMALITY:

Normality of a solution may be defined as the number of gram equivalent weights of solute in 1 litre of solution.

PROCEDURE:

To prepare 0.1M of glucose solution (250 ml)

Molarity = <u>no. of moles</u>

Volume of solvent (L)

Molarity = weight/molecular weight x volume (L)

Weight = Molarity x mol. mass .{Vol(ml)/1000}

Weight of glucose to prepare 0.1M glucose (250 ml) = 0.1x180x250/1000 = 4.5%

PRECAUTIONS:

Heat is evolved when NaOH is added to water. So preparation of solution is handled with care.

Lower meniscus while making up the volume in volumetric flask should be considered.

Final volume is made up after the solute is completely is completely dissolved in little amount of water.

CHAPTER THREE

EXPERIMENT NO. 2

AIM: Normal value of constituents in biological fluids.
Blood Values:
Haematocrit:
Men 38-54%
Women 36-47%

1. **Haemoglobin:**

    Men 14-18 g%
    Women 12-16 g%
    Child 12-14 g%
    New born 14.5-24.5 g%

1. **Blood Counts:**

    Erythrocytes (men) 4.5-6 x 106
    Erythrocytes (women) 4.3-5.5 x 106
    Leucocytes (total) 5000-10000 (100%)
    Lymphocytes 1000-4000 (20-40%)
    Eosinophiles 50-300 (1-3%)
    Basophils 0-100 (0.1%)
    Monocytes 200-800 (4-8%)
    Platelets 200000-500000

3. **Standard Values in Blood:**

    Acetone, serum 0.3-2 mg/100 ml
    Alpha amino nitrogen, plasma 3.5-5 mg/100 ml

Calcium, serum (total) 9-11 mg/100 ml
Cholesterol, serum (total) 150-250 mg/100 ml
Fibrinogen, plasma 200-400 mg/100 ml
Glucose (fasting) blood 60-100 mg/100 ml
Iron (serum) 75-175 mg/100 ml
Lipid (total) serum 450-850 mg/100 ml
Proteins, serum (total) 6.8 gm/100 ml
Albumin 3.5-5.5 g/100 ml

4. **Normal Urine Value:**

Acetone 0
Alpha amino nitrogen 64-199 mg/24 hrs
Ammonia 20-70 Eq/L
Calcium <150 mg/L
Creatinine 15-25 mg/kg body weight/24hrs
Protein (albumin) 10-100 mg/24 hrs
Urea nitrogen 6-17 g/24 hrs
pH 6.0

CHAPTER FOUR

EXPERIMENT NO. 3

AIM: To perform calibration of pH electrode.

REQUIREMENTS: Standard buffer, tablets of pH 4, 7 and 9, pH meter, distilled water.

PRINCIPLE: pH electrode consists of thin porous membrane sealed at the end of hard glass tube containing 0.1M HCl into which is immersed a silver wire coated with silver chloride. This silver-silver chloride (Ag/AgCl) electrode acts as an internal reference that generates a constant potential. The principle of operation of pH electrode based on the fact that if there is a gradient of hydrogen ions activity across membrane, this will generate a potential.

PROCEDURE:

1. Calibration is carried out using standard buffer of pH 4, 7 and 9.
2. The standard buffer is prepared by dissolving the respective buffer tablets in 100 ml distilled water.
3. The clear and blotted dry electrode was immersed in the standard buffer solution with pH 4, allowed to equilibrate and the pH meter was adjusted to the known pH value.
4. This process is then repeated with the second buffer solution.

PRECAUTIONS:

1. The glass membrane of pH electrode is fragile and easily damaged. It is important that its surface remains hydrated and so it should be kept immersed in water when not in use.
2. Adequate equilibrium time should be allowed before adjusting the pH value.

EXPERIMENT NO. 4

AIM: To detect the presence of monosaccharide with the help of Molish's reagent.

REQUIREMENTS: Molish reagent, burners, test tubes, water bath, conc. H_2SO_4

PRINCIPLE:

Glucose conc. H_2SO_4 hydroxymethyl furfural

Pentose conc. H_2SO_4 furfural

This reaction is due to the formation of furfural and furfural derivative in case of hexose hydroxymethyl furfural is formed by the action of conc. H_2SO_4 and in case of pentose, furfural is formed by the action of conc. H_2SO_4. H_2SO_4 acts as dehydrating agent. Hydroxymethyl furfural is very reactive and it condenses with alpha naphthol to give a violet colored ring. This is given by furfural and all ferfurol leading substances. So it is not a specific test for carbohydrates.

PROCEDURE: Take 5 ml of test solution in test tubes and add 2 drops of Molish reagent and mix it thoroughly. Incline the tube and along the tube add about 3 ml conc. H_2SO_4 and allow it to flow down the side of the test tube, thus forming a layer of acid. A violet ring formed at the junction of two liquids indicates presence of carbohydrates.

PRECAUTIONS:

1. Use test tube holder while pouring conc. H_2SO_4.
2. Do not pour more conc. H_2SO_4 otherwise the ring will dissolve and it appears black.
3. Do not shake after ring formation.

CHAPTER SIX

EXPERIMENT NO. 5

AIM: To study the properties of carbohydrate with the help of Fehling's solution.

REQUIREMENTS: Fehling solution A (Copper sulphate), Fehling solution B (Na-K tartarate and KOH), conical flask, pipette, sugar solution.

PRINCIPLE: Monosaccharide possessing a free aldehyde or ketone group have the properties of readily reducing the ions of certain metals such as Cu, Bi, Fe, Hg, etc. The sugars in turn are oxidized to a mixture of sugar acids. Fehling's solution contains alkali which acts on sugar molecule and form enediols (two OH group attached to a double bond carbon system). The enediols are very unstable and therefore highly reactive. They can reduce metallic ions and in Fehling's solution reduce Cu++, which combines with OH to form Coppr hydroxide, which gives a red ppt. of Copper oxide upon heating. When blue Copper hydroxide is suspended in absence of reducing agent it is converted into black CuO.

PRECAUTIONS:

1. We should heat the test tubes carefully.
2. We should put the solution drop by drop in the test tube, so that we will obtain correct results.
3. We should handle the instruments carefully.

CHAPTER SEVEN

EXPERIMENT NO. 6

AIM: To detect the presence of reducing sugar with the help of Benedict's reagent.

REQUIREMENT: Test tubes, Benedict's reagent, sugar solution, burner.

PRINCIPLE: Carbohydrates with the free aldehyde or ketone groups have reducing properties in alkaline solution. In addition monosaccharide acts as reducing agents in weakly acidic solution. Benedict's reagent contains sodium citrate, sodium carbonate and copper sulphate solution. Reducing sugar reduces the Cu^{++} ion to Cu^{+} ion and finally forms insoluble brick red ppt. in a solution containing reducing sugar.

PROCEDURE: Take 2.0 ml of Benedict's reagent. To it 2.0 ml of test solution is added. The mixture was mixed very well and heated in boiling water bath for 3 minutes.

PRECAUTIONS:

1. The test tube should be cleaned before starting the experiment.
2. Add sufficient amount of Benedict's reagent and sugar solution.
3. Heat the test tube carefully.

CHAPTER EIGHT

EXPERIMENT NO. 7

AIM: To detect the presence of monosaccharide using Barfoed's reagent.

REQUIREMENTS: Two test tubes, burner, water bath, Barfoed reagents, droppers.

PRINCIPLE: Unlike monosaccharides, disaccharides are non-reducing agents and i.e. do not reduce the cupric ions of Barfoed solution in acidic solution. However, on prolong heating disaccharide also respond to this test because the acetic acid present in Barfoed solution hydrolyses disaccharide to monosaccharide. Barfoed test is a Copper detection test and reduce Cupric to Cuperous but differs from Benedict's test in the medium of reduction. Here it is brought in acidic medium where as Benedict's is brought in alkaline medium.

PROCEDURE: Take 2.0 ml of Barfoed reagent and add4 drops of test solution and boil for 1 minute.

PRECAUTION:

1. Use test tube holders while heating.
2. Heating process should be properly done, so that change in color will be observed.

CHAPTER NINE

EXPERIMENT NO. 8

AIM: Identification and separation of amino acid by Thin layer Chromatography (TLC).

REQUIREMENTS: Whatmann's no. 1 filter paper, capillary tube, sprayer, Petri plate, chromatographic chamber, hot air oven.

PRINCIPLE: Amino acid is separated based on their distribution coefficient between stationary and liquid mobile phase. Amino acids with higher solubility in stationary phase move slowly as compared to those with higher solubility in mobile phase. The separated amino acids are detected by spraying ninhydrin reagent. All amino acids give purple or bluish purple color on reaction with ninhydrin except prolin and hydroxyproline, which gives a yellow coloured product. The reaction leads to the formation of purple complexes.

Solvent System: Mobile phase- n-butanol : acetic acid : water (4:1:5)- Prepare the solvent system by mixing 40.0 ml of n-butanol, 10.0 ml of acetic acid and 50.0 ml of water in a separating funnel. Use proper organic layer as mobile phase.

Ninhydrin reagent: Dissolve 100 mg of ninhydrin in 100 ml of n-butanol.

Standard amino acid: Prepare 10 ml of individual amino acid solutions (4 mg/ml) using distilled water.

PROCEDURE:

1. Take microscope slide as a supporting material and spread slurry of silica gel over it to form a thin layer. Allow it to dry and activate it by placing in oven set at 105°C temp. for 30 min.
2. Spot the amino acid and sample at the origin with the help of a capillary tube. The diameter of the sample spotted should not exceed 3-4 mm.

3. Place the plate in the chromatographic chamber having the mobile phase. Run it for 1 hr.
4. After the run, TLC is removed, the solvent front is marked using a pencil and air dry at room temperature.
5. Spray the ninhydrin reagent on the plate and transfer it to an oven at 80-90 °C for few minutes.
6. Alpha amino acid show purple color while praline gives yellow color. Outline the spots with a pencil.
7. Measure the distance in cm from the origin to the center of the outline spot and calculate the R_f value for the separated amino acids and standard amino acid using the formula-

R_f value = $\dfrac{\text{Distance traveled by amino acid}}{\text{Distance traveled by mobile phase}}$

PRECAUTIONS:

1. Hold the TLC at the tip.
2. Mark carefully on the paper.
3. Dip the lower tip of the TLC in the solvent below the margin.
4. Loading of sample should be done carefully.
5. Do not disturb the TLC and the solvent during the experiment.

CHAPTER TEN

EXPERIMENT NO. 9

AIM: Identification and separation of Plant pigments by Paper Chromatography.

REQUIREMENTS: Green spinach leaves, pestle and mortar, Whatmann's no. 1 filter paper, capillary tube, benzene : acetone (85:15).

PRINCIPLE: Plant pigments are separated on the basis of differences in their partition coefficient in a binary solvent system. The pigment with higher affinity for stationary phase move slowly as compared to those with higher affinity for mobile phase.

Extract Preparation:

1. Homogenize the leaves (approx 1 gm) in the pestle and mortar in 10 ml 80% chilled acetone. Add a pinch of Sodium carbonate to avoid the destruction of chlorophylloids.
2. Filter the extract through Whatmann No.1 filter paper and collect in the flask or centrifuge the solution and use supernatant for separation of pigments.

PROCEDURE:

1. Take Whatmann No.1 filter paper. Cut it into thin strips of required length.
2. Draw a line across the filter paper with a lead pencil at a distance of 2 to 2.5 cm from one edge and put a dot at the centre of the line.
3. With the help of a micropipette apply spot of the sample on the mark at the centre of this line. The size of the spot should be as small as possible. The wet sample spot should be dried before applying additional aliquot and this process is repeated 10 times.

4. Hang the filter paper in chromatographic chamber containing the mobile phase.
5. Allow the mobile phase to run down the paper till the solvent front reaches the required length.
6. Remove the paper and mark the solvent front with lead pencil and let it dry at room temperature.
7. Measure the distance of solvent front from the base line.
8. Calculate the Rf values of different pigment as follows-

$$R_f \text{ value} = \frac{\text{Distance traveled by the sample}}{\text{Distance traveled by solvent front}}$$

1. Identify the different pigments in the mixture by comparing their Rf values with those of the reference standard.

PRECAUTIONS:

1. Hold the chromatographic paper at the tip.
2. Mark carefully on the paper.
3. Dip the lower tip of the paper in the solvent below the margin.

CHAPTER ELEVEN

EXPERIMENT NO.10

AIM: To estimate the protein content in bovine serum albumin (BSA) by Bradford method.

REQUIREMENTS: Standard bovine serum albumin (5 mg/ml) solution, Comassie brilliant blue (CBBG250), ortho-phosphoric acid, 90% ethanol and colorimeter.

PRINCIPLE: The Bradford assay is a rapid, simple, inexpensive, sensitive method for the estimation of protein in a sample. It is based on the observation that the absorbance maximum for an acidic of comassie brilliant blue G250 shifts from 465 nm to 595 nm when binding to protein occurs. Both hydrophobic and ionic interactions stabilize the ionic form of dyes causing the visible color change, which can be measured at 595 nm. Thus from the absorbance at 595 nm the amount of protein in the sample solution can be quantitatively estimated.

Preparation of reagents (CBBG 250): Dissolve 0.25 gm of CBBG 250 in 1N 100 ml of ortho-phosphoric acid. Insoluble partials in Bradford reagent is filtered by using Whatmann's filter paper.

PROCEDURE:

1. Take bovine serum albumin standard solution in a test tube as 0.4, 0.81.2, 1.6 and 2.0 ml aliquots.
2. Make up the volume of each test tube to 2.0 ml with distilled water.
3. Add 5.0 ml of Bradford reagent in each test tube.
4. Keep the teat tube for 20 to 30 min at room temperature.
5. Take the absorbance at 595 nm.
6. Draw standard curve of bovine serum albumin and find the concentration of unknown sample.

PRECAUTIONS:

1. The volume of bovine serum albumin and Comassie brilliant blue must be measured accurately.
2. The reading of colorimeter must be set at zero for blank reading initially.

CHAPTER TWELVE

EXPERIMENT NO. 11

AIM: Estimation of the amount of reducing sugar in the unknown sample by DNS method.

INTRODUCTION: Monosaccharides are the building blocks of oligosaccharides and polysaccharides. They contain highly reactive carbonyl group which is the powerful reducing agent. The carbohydrates containing aldehyde and ketonic group are called as aldoses and ketoses, respectively. The carbonyl function of sugar undergoes isomerization to form 1,2 dienol. Dienols are also reducing species and can reduce metallic ions, therefore, when monosaccharides are heated with alkaline solution of cuprous ions it is reduced to cupric ions. It further gets precipitated as cupric oxide.

PRINCIPLE: Reducing sugars react with Dinitrosalicylic acid reagent in analkaline boiling medium, which on boiling gives an orange-yellow coloured complex, which is measured at 540 nm. During this process, 3, 5 Dinitrosalicylate is reduced to 5-amino, 3-nitrosalicylic acid.

REQUIREMENTS:

1. Standard glucose solution- 40mg of glucose is dissolved in 100ml of distilled water to get a standard solution of 400 microgram/ml.
2. Disnitosalicylate reagent- 2gm of 3,5 dinitrosalicylic acid is suspended in 40ml. of 2 N NaOH. To this 100ml of 60% sodium potassium tartarate solution is added. The final volume is made up to 200ml using distilled water. The reagent is filtered and stored in dark coloured bottles.
3. Test tubes, pipettes, boiling water bath, colorimeter.

PROCEDURE:
Different aliquots of standard glucose solution (400 µg/ml) ranging from 0.2-1.0 ml are pipetted into test tubes. The final volume is made up to 2

ml with distilled water. 0.5 ml of 3, 5 Dinitrosalicylic acid reagent is added to all the tubes. The tubes are incubated in a boiling water bath for 10 minutes and then cooled to room temperature. Finally, 2.5 ml of distilled water is added to all the tubes. The intensity of the colour developed is measured in terms of optical density using a blank at 540 nm in a colorimeter.

The absorbance on Y-axis and the amount of sugar in µg on x-axis is plotted to obtain a standard curve. The standard line passing through a maximum number of points is plotted in line with the origin.

2.Estimation of reducing sugar in peas:

One gram of fresh peas are weighed and homogenized with known amount of distilled water in ice cold condition. The homogenate is centrifuged at 3000 rpm for 10 min. 0.1 ml of pea extract is taken for estimation of reducing sugars by similar method as for standard solutions.

PRECAUTIONS:

1. Accurate volume of standard solutions for preparation of standard curve should be taken.
2. The reading of colorimeter must be set at zero initially for blank reading.

CHAPTER THIRTEEN

EXPERIMENT NO. 12

AIM: Estimation of the amount of protein in the unknown sample by Lowry method.

PRINCIPLE: Peptide bond in polypeptide chain reacts with alkaline $CuSO_4$ to give blue coloured complex. Aromatic amino acids like tyrosne and tryptophan residues of protein causes reduction of phosphomolybdate and phosphotungstate component of Folin's reagent to give bluish products, measured at 670 nm.

REAGENTS:

1. Reagent A: 2% sodium carbonate in a 0.1 N NaOH.
2. Reagent B: 0.5% Copper sulphate in Sodium-Potassium tartarate (1%)
3. Reagent C: Alkaline copper reagent is prepared by mixing 50 ml of reagent A with 10 ml of reagent B
4. Folin's Reagent- 1 N
5. Bovine Serum Albumin: A standard stock solution of BSA was prepared by weighing 50 mg of albumin and made upto 100ml with 0.9% saline for 500 microgram per ml stock.

PROCEDURE:

Different volumes of stock standard 0.2, 0.4, 0.6, 0.8 and 1.0 (100, 200, 300, 400, 500 microgram respectively) were pipetted in different test-tubes. 0.5 ml of unknown solution was also taken in separate tube. Solutions in all tubes were made upto 1 ml using distilled water. A blank containing 1ml distilled water was also taken. 5 ml of reagent C was added to all the test tubes, mixed well and kept for 10 min at room temperature. 0.5 ml of Folin's reagent was added to all the test tubes and allowed to stand for 30 minutes at room temperature after mixing. Then Optical density was measured in a colorimeter at 670nm.

A graph is plotted with the concentration of standard solution on X-axis and optical density along Y axis. The amount of albumin in the test solution is read from the graph.

PRECAUTIONS:

1. Accurate volume of standard solutions for preparation of standard curve should be taken.
2. The reading of colorimeter must be set at zero initially for blank reading

CHAPTER FOURTEEN

EXPERIMENT NO. 13

AIM: Estimation of the amount of protein in the unknown sample by Biuret method.

PRINCIPLE: Peptide bond in polypeptide chain reacts with alkaline $CuSO_4$ to give blue coloured complex.

REAGENTS:

1. Biuret reagent : 3.0 g Copper sulphate and 9 g Sodium-Potassium tartarate in 500 ml of 0.2mol per litre sodium hydroxide.
2. Bovine Serum Albumin: A standard stock solution of BSA was prepared by weighing 1g of albumin and made upto 50ml with 0.1N sodium hydroxide (20 mg per ml).

PROCEDURE:

Different volumes of stock standard 0.2, 0.4, 0.6, 0.8 and 1.0 (4000, 8000, 12000, 16000, 20000 microgram respectively) were pipetted in different test-tubes. 0.5 ml of unknown solution was also taken in separate tube. Solutions in all tubes were made upto 1 ml using distilled water. A blank containing 1ml distilled water was also taken. 5 ml of biuret reagent was added to all the test tubes, mixed well and kept for 10 min at 37oC. Then Optical density was measured in a colorimeter at 540nm.

A graph is plotted with the concentration of standard solution on X-axis and optical density along Y axis. The amount of albumin in the test solution is read from the graph. The amount of albumin in whole of given solution was then calculated.

PRECAUTIONS:

1. Accurate volume of standard solutions for preparation of standard curve should be taken.

2. The reading of colorimeter must be set at zero initially for blank reading

CHAPTER FIFTEEN

CHAPTER SIXTEEN

EXPERIMENT NO.15

AIM: Estimation of the amount of DNA in the unknown sample by DPA method.

PRINCIPLE: estimation is based on quantitative reaction between deoxypentose sugar and Diphenylamine reagent. Intensity of coloured formed is measured with spectrophotometry. Under extreme acidic conditions, DNA usually denature quantitavily followed by dehydration of deoxy sugar to β-hydroxy butaldehyde. This in acidic medium condenses with DPA to produce deep blue coloured product which has absorption at 590 nm.

REAGENTS:

1. Diphenylamine reagent: 0 g of Diphenylamine in 100 ml of glacial acetic acid and 2.5 ml of conc.sulphuric acid.containing 0.5 g of ferric chloride.
2. Standard DNA solution: A standard stock solution of DNA was prepared by dissolving 50mg of DNA in 100 ml of saline citrate. (500 microgram per ml).
3. Saline citrate: 0.15M NaCl with 0.015M Sodium citrate.

PROCEDURE:

Different volumes of stock standard 0.2, 0.4, 0.6, 0.8 and 1.0 (100, 200, 300, 400, 500 microgram respectively) were pipetted in different test-tubes. 0.5 ml of unknown solution was also taken in separate tube. Solutions in all tubes were made upto 1ml with distilled water. A blank containing 1.0 ml using was also taken. 2 ml of DPA reagent was added to all the test tubes, mixed well and kept for 10 min in a boiling water bath. After cooling Then Optical density was measured in a colorimeter at 590nm.

A graph is plotted with the concentration of standard solution on X-axis and optical density along Y axis. The amount of DNA in the test solution is read from the graph. The amount of DNA in whole of given solution was then calculated.

PRECAUTIONS:

1. Accurate volume of standard solutions for preparation of standard curve should be taken.
2. The reading of colorimeter must be set at zero initially for blank reading